TRAGEDY *at* SEA

TRAGEDY
at SEA

William S. Butler

Douglas Keeney

BKF

Mishaps at sea make good photographs and great tales, but since 1790 the United States Coast Guard has tried valiantly to keep these mishaps from becoming tragedies. To an outstanding degree they have been successful in that effort. The publishers salute and thank the men and women of The United States Coast Guard for their dedication and professionalism as "keepers of the sea."

ISBN 1-884532-17-9

All photos courtesy of The United States Coast Guard
Our thanks to Robert M. Browning Jr. and Scott T. Price for their assistance in the publication of this book.

Printed in Canada

Published by Butler+Keeney+Farmer
3900 Shelbyville Road
Louisville, Kentucky 40207
502•895•3939

CONTENTS

INTRODUCTION

"For all the celebrations it has been the object of in prose and song, the sea has never been friendly to Man." *Joseph Conrad*

Man is neither fowl nor fish, yet he rules the skies and seas by the wonderful employment of technology. We fly; we sail.

The ease with which we use our knowledge, hard-won over thousands of years, to overcome Nature's limitations gives us satisfaction today, but it also gives us a false sense of security. Our notions of sovereignty are periodically shattered when our technology fails and the unimpeded power of Nature finds an opening and cascades death and destruction all around. Planes fall out of the sky, and ships sink.

The ocean is a vast arena in which the force of Nature is always vying with Man's agent—the ship. There may be days when the sea is on its best behavior, but—ask any sailor—even a placid sea can kill you. Water is inimical to us. We cannot breath it nor walk on it. The sheer size of it makes it a lethal element. In fact, it is a prodigious act of confidence that we set to sea at all. It is at best a calculated risk, despite the size and sophistication of Man's hardware, and experienced merchant

Top photo: The 86-foot shrimp trawler John and Olaf *was spotted aground near Jute Bay, Kodiak Island, by Coast Guard aircraft. The crew had abandoned her after a severe storm on the night of January 16, 1974. It took only three days of exposure for the boat to look like this.*

Bottom photo: A Japan Airlines airplane ditches in the Pacific.

mariners know better than anyone that damage and death is just a little bad luck away.

But we are drawn to the sea for many reasons.

The global delivery of goods is primarily a maritime affair. The oceans are the world's highways for commerce, and are charted and organized down to the last mile.

Much of the world feeds itself from the bounty of the sea, and uncountable numbers of fishing vessels roam vast stretches of open water hunting and gathering the ocean's offerings.

And millions of people enjoy the oceans recreationally, sailing or being sailed from port to port, immersing themselves emotionally in the rescucitative powers of the water and wind.

But for every ten people whose experience at sea has been trouble-free, there is one who has come up hard against the furies that have plagued sailors for centuries.

First, there is weather. At sea there can be storms of such ferocity that there are no land-based equivalents. It is nature gone wild, wilder than the imagination can conjure, and the volume of water and wind a hurricane can generate can break a ship the size of a skyscraper in half. It has happened many times. And when

Top photo: 430 miles northwest of Achill Head, Ireland, in October 1965, the Swedish freighter Orion *radioed that she had three cracks in her decks from heavy seas. The U.S. Coast Guard cutter* Northwind *stood by to help while the ship plowed through stormy weather on the way to Toledo, Ohio, USA.*

Bottom photo: Rescue helicopter basket-hoists three men to safety from the deck of the grounded fishing trawler Oriental *in December 1969. The ship foundered and broke up in heavy surf on the Outer Banks near Nags Head, North Carolina.*

a ship goes down in a storm there is no hope save a lifeboat, and a lifeboat will not survive a force that snapped a 10,000-ton tanker in two like a dry twig. The merchant mariner's nightmare, fate's cruelest joke, is the "thousand mile swim"; treading water in a trackless ocean as the ship that was your home slides beneath the waves. What can you do but say your prayers, curse the darkness, and find something to float on?

Then there is fire. There is no such thing as a trivial fire on a ship. The meagerest spark is cause for alarm, because a burning ship is nothing more than a floating oven. When fire consumes the deck on which you are standing, there is no place to go but the water, and the water will not save you.

Then there is the grinding, shuddering sensation that tells you that you are not floating anymore; that something solid—a reef, rocks, a sandbar, an iceberg, even the shore—has grabbed the underside of the ship. There are no good results from this. The ship is crippled at the least, and dead at the worst, sinking from an unrepairable gash in the belly or stranded high and dry on the shore.

Finally there are the inevitable collisions of moving objects, when fate puts two ships on an opposing course, and neither radar nor the pilots detect the tragic intersection until it is too late.

When these emergencies and tragedies happen at sea, there is often nowhere to turn but to each man's ingenuity, bravery, and skill. But the world's maritime services, including the United States Coast Guard, have an old and rich tradition of being the saviors of the sea. Their heroics are the stuff of legends, and wherever sea tales are told there is unstinting praise for the sea services and the men and women who put their lives on the line for fellow sailors.

The pictures ahead are stirring testimony to their courage.

Left: The ill-fated Argo
Merchant *(see pages 18-21).*

The Coast Guard cutter Citrus *cannot save the burning ship* Pacific Star.

The Army transport ship Joseph P. Connoly *abandoned and adrift in the North Atlantic, January 1948.*

AGROUND

March 1947. An easterly gale strikes with full force on the *SS Oakey Alexander* as she steams near Cape Elizabeth, Maine. The ship goes aground on the rocks near the Cape; it is only a matter of time until the ship is torn in half not far from the shore.

The tugboat *Troy* was towing the dredge *Titan* and a 180-foot barge when its towline became entangled in the propeller. The line severed and the dredge, barge, and towboat drifted helplessly until they wound up on a sand bar several hundred feet off the shore. As the tide came in, the towboat sank as swells came over the side, and the dredge and barge pushed closer to the beach. 15,000 gallons of oil on the barge and 5,000 gallons on the towboat gave the Coast Guard some cause for alarm. Salvors were called in to anchor the dredge and barge until the oil could be off-loaded.

Nine men were rescued from the tug and dredge.

Left: The dredge and barge are pummeled by incoming waves as they sit just offshore.

Right, top and bottom: Wet-suited salvors secure lines to the Troy, *which has sunk up to the roofline of the wheelhouse. The* Troy *was later removed as a navigational hazard.*

December 21, 1976. Despite six days of efforts to save the *Argo Merchant*, building seas and high wintry winds break the 18,743-ton tanker in half. The 644-foot tanker was bound for Salem, Massachusetts with a cargo of over seven million gallons of heavy industrial fuel oil when she ran aground on December 15, twenty-eight miles southeast of Nantucket Island in international waters. Storms and heavy seas had caused the tanker to stray eighteen miles off course into the Nantucket Shoals.

Coast Guard efforts to save the ship centered on dewatering the flooded engine room. The oil spill that resulted from the breakup became the Coast Guard's top priority when saving the engine room was fruitless.

The Coast Guard Air Station, Cape Cod, Massachusetts dispatched helicopters to rescue the thirty-eight crew members. The last man was lifted to safety on December 16.

Left: The Argo Merchant's *decks are awash from heavy seas, as the ship wallows aground near Nantucket Island.*

Above: The Argo Merchant *is hammered by raging seas, and it is a matter of time before she breaks up. The weight of the cargo prevents the ship from floating free, and creates tremendous torque forces on the hull.*

Right: During rescue operations, an HH-3F helicopter from the Coast Guard Station on Cape Cod hovers over the stricken Liberian-registered tanker. It took two days to airlift all thirty-eight crewmen to safety. Airlift operations also brought in dewatering pumps to the tanker, along with the Coast Guard's Atlantic Strike Force team. Although the ship has not severed at this point, the hull is cracked, and the stern is sinking fast.

Left: Sections of the broken-apart Argo Merchant remain on the surface. The seas have calmed, but the damage has been done. Nearly eight million gallons of industrial fuel oil have spilled from the ruptured holds.

Right and below: The bow arches toward the sky, then slips beneath the waves. The oil from the tanker caused one of America's first ecological disasters.

Visitors to the Statue of Liberty in New York were treated to an extra attraction in May of 1957. A sightseeing boat, the *City of Keansburg*, ran aground in the shallow water around the island. The Coast Guard cutters *Manitou* and *Tuckahoe*, a police launch, and a commercial tug rushed in to assist. The 150 passengers were ready to debark the ship, but the rising tide refloated it quickly.

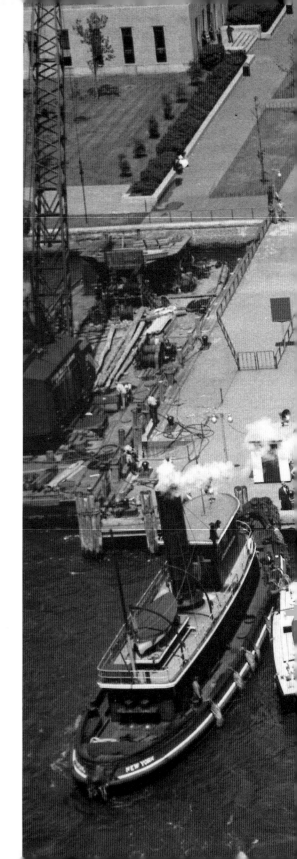

The Maltese-registered *Eldia*, a 471-foot, 9800 ton oil tanker, came ashore near Nauset Beach, Cape Cod, in a ferocious northeast storm, March 29, 1984. Twenty-three crew members, all Filipinos, were rescued by Coast Guard helicopters flying in marginal conditions during the storm.

The ship was returning to Norfolk, Virginia from St. Johns, New Brunswick when sixty-foot seas whipped up by twenty-knot winds caused the ship to go off course. By the time sea anchors were deployed, the ship was already in the surf line and out of control. The ship came to rest on the shore at Nauset Beach, where residents quickly notified police and fire departments.

After shore crews stabilized the vessel, its cargo of oil was offloaded and re-placed by seawater as ballast to keep the ship stable. Salvage procedures were put in place by the ship's owners, but in the meantime the ship itself became Cape Cod's biggest tourist attraction.

Left and below: The Russian freighter Uzbekistan *went aground near Pachena Point near Vancouver, British Columbia on April 2, 1943. Strong currents and a heavy fog drove the ship to the shore, where a receding tide left the vessel high and dry. Because of the ruggedness and inaccessibility of the area, the ship was not salvaged, but given up for lost.*

The diesel-powered coastal tanker *Mary A. Whelan* lies trapped on a sand bar at the end of the jetty at Rockaway Point Breakwater, New York. The tanker ran aground at 10 p.m. December 23, 1968 while en route with her cargo of oil to Nassau County. Below-freezing temperatures and thirty mile-per-hour winds snapped the lines of tugs attempting to pull the vessel free. After three days of effort, the cargo of oil was transferred to another ship, and at high tide the ship was refloated and towed to a Brooklyn shipyard for repairs.

The tanker *Ocean Eagle* ran aground at the mouth of the San Juan, Puerto Rico harbor channel on March 3, 1968, spilling oil that washed high on the tourist beaches of Isla De Cabras. More than two million gallons of South American crude oil spilled from the tanker. The Greek crew was rescued by tugboats in the area. Above, the stricken ship has clearly broken in half, but has not separated. At right, a U.S. Navy destroyer escort enters the port of San Juan for weekend leave. All eyes are on the *Ocean Eagle*'s stern section, which, after breaking off, is still leaking oil onto the resort beaches.

A month after the grounding, the *Ocean Eagle* still lies on a shelf on the west side of the San Juan harbor channel. At left, looking from the fortress of El Morro Castle, the broken halves of the ship face in different directions. The bow section at right shows the ship's original heading.

March 1956. A nor'easter packing high winds, blizzard snows, and high sea swells pushed the Italian freighter *SS Etrusco* aground in the backyards of homes on Scituate Beach, Massachusetts near the North Jetty Light Station.

After ten hours in the grounded ship just 200 yards from shore, the captain and his crew of 29 were brought safely to land, despite 22-degree temperatures and zero visibility caused by 60-knot wind-driven snow.

The *Etrusco* was bound from Germany to East Boston to pick up grain for delivery to Rumania.

The **Margaret Rose**, *a fishing vessel, lies on the beach near Wood End Light near Provincetown, Massachusetts on January 16, 1962. The ship ran aground and was caught in the surf line at Race Point. A Coast Guard amphibious vessel at right assisted the rescue of the seven men aboard.*

The fishing boat O.M.Arnold *was washed high on the rocks by a storm off the coast of Alaska. The ship was not damaged severely, and was floated on the high tide by a Coast Guard cutter.*

IN FLAMES

A mid-ships blaze aboard the $27 million luxury liner *Cunard Ambassador* caused all crew members to abandon ship on September 13, 1974, leaving the smoldering ship to wallow abandoned some thirty-five miles off Key West.

The 480-foot liner was sailing with no passengers en route from Miami to New York, where it was to pick up travelers for a cruise to Veracruz, Mexico. The fire was caused when fuel from a ruptured line splashed on the hot diesel engines and ignited.

All but fifty-three of the 309 crew members were transferred from the ship to a passing naval tanker. The remainder joined forty Coast Guardsmen in fighting the blaze.

The fire was not successfully put out, however, and water pumped into the ship began to cause the ship to list seven degrees. Further efforts brought the blaze under control on the second day.

The *Ambassador*, its white exterior scorched by intense heat, was soon towed to a mooring near Key West where Lloyds of London was to determine the extent of the damage.

Part of the crew from the Ambassador *man the lifeboats.*

A passing naval tanker, the Tallulah, *picks up the crew.*

Coast Guard firemen battled the blaze; one was injured from smoke damage to the eyes.

November 8, 1956. An electrical fire sets the fishing trawler *AGDA* ablaze off Montauk Point, Long Island, New York. Assisting in the rescue was the U.S. Navy submarine *Dogfish*, and the destroyer *Willis A. Lee*, along with Coast Guard cutters and airplanes. Another fishing vessel, the *Seahawk,* assisted in removing the crew.

Two thousand gallons of fuel ignited on the *AGDA*, but no one was injured. The ship, however, could not be saved and sank five hours after the fire began.

Left: A Coast Guard Albatross amphibian plane (pontoon visible at upper part of the photograph) coordinates rescue efforts as the Dogfish *eases her way to the burning boat.*

Right: The Willis A. Lee *aims its bow fire hoses on the* AGDA, *but the ship is burning out of control. The ship's crew has already been transferred to a whaler.*

The fire aboard the Prinsendam *is out of control. Heat from the blaze below decks has blistered and burned the outer hull.*

October 1980. As the Holland Cruise ship *Prinsendam* steamed through the Gulf of Alaska with 320 passengers and 200 crew members, enroute from Vancouver to Singapore, a fire of unknown origin broke out. A fuel line may have split and sprayed diesel fuel on hot pipes in the engine room. Whatever its origin, the fire knocked out the electrical system, shutting down the water pumps used for fire-fighting. Crewmen used hand-held carbon dioxide fire extinguishers, but the fire spread to other parts of the ship.

All passengers and crew escaped the ship in lifeboats on the captain's orders. The seas were rough, the winds blowing some thirty knots, and the weather was frigid. For hours the survivors drifted in the lifeboats, some becoming hypothermic.

Three Coast Guard ships and the U.S. Supertanker *Williamsburgh* arrived on the scene. Coast Guard helicopters maneuvered through strong winds to lift the survivors to rescue ships.

The *Prinsendam* was towed to port a few days later when the fire was out and cold.

Right: Smoke pours from the Prinsendam's *midsection as crewmen try to contain the fire with small fire extinguishers.*

A U.S. Coast Guard HH-3 helo hovers over the burning cruise ship.

The starboard list of the damaged ship is very noticeable as it is being towed to port. The lowering ropes from the lifeboat davits hang from both sides of the ship.

A Coast Guard HH-3 helicopter surveys the scorched upper decks of the **Prinsendam.** *A motor launch hangs from a port side davit as the ship is towed through calmer seas than on the day of the fire.*

The center of the Prinsendam's *superstructure and its bridge are totally burned out.*

The blistered hull is a typical result of a severe below-decks fire. A metal ship on fire radiates tremendous heat.

Crewmen on the Coast Guard buoy tender *Gentian* (left) make preparations to fight a fire as they approach the burning fishing boat *Shannon* thirty-five miles off the coast of New Jersey on December 15, 1954. Before the Coast Guard arrival, the five *Shannon* crew members were safely picked up by the passing trawler *South Seas*.

Like other Coast Guard vessels, the *Gentian* was configured for fire-fighting. Its fire hoses tried desperately to control the blaze with foam spray, but the *Shannon* was too far gone to save. She burned to her waterline quite quickly and sank, (above) leaving only strewn debris on the surface of the ocean.

August, 1970. Off the California coast, the Philippine merchant vessel *Don Jose Figueras* is seriously afire (left) below decks. Life rafts, one of which has its canopy up, can be seen off the starboard side. At right, a severe ten percent list to starboard can be seen, as the fire has the ship dead in the water.

A U.S. Navy ship, the *Perseus*, picked up and transported the crewmen to San Francisco. There were no casualties.

Collision damage on the Keytrader.

Coast Guard boat aims water from its bow hoses on the burning ships. Oil and fuel burns both on the ships and on the water.

The American tanker *Keytrader* collided with the Norwegian freighter *Baune* in a thick fog as both approached the mouth of the Mississippi River, seventy-five miles south of New Orleans. The *Keytrader* and the *Baune* burst into flames on impact. The *Keytrader* was carrying 18,000 tons of gasoline and other flammables from a Shell oil refinery. Coast Guard units rescued sixty-one crew members from both ships. After the fire was brought under control, there were five confirmed deaths and eleven more men missing and presumed dead.

Even after the fire was out, Coast Guard helicopters brought in and applied over 10,000 gallons of foam to cool the hull of the *Keytrader*.

Right: Coast Guard firemen lay water on burning fuel as they wade ankle deep in fire retardant foam on the deck.

November 1984. The tanker *Puerto Rican* is rocked by a mysterious explosion at 3:25 a.m. off the California coast, south of the Farallon Islands. The blast tore the tanker into two sections; the stern sank in 2400 feet of water, while the bow remained afloat. After the fire was extinguished, the bow was tethered so that inspectors from the Coast Guard could investigate the cause of the blast.

The explosion was immediately suspicious to the ship's owners, the Coast Guard, and the FBI because of numerous threats against the ship in the preceding few days. The ownership had been fighting with a union over a new contract, and specific threats of a "fire bombing" had been made by anonymous callers.

Sabotage was only one of the possible causes of the blast. Maritime explosion experts guessed on first investigation that a volatile concentration of petrochemical vapor might have been the culprit. Damage, they found, was not consistent with damage normally associated with explosive devices. There were unconfirmed reports that more than one explosion occurred, tearing a 100-foot steel section of the deck free and folding it toward the bow. The *Puerto Rican*'s millions of gallons of oil were relatively intact, but bunker oil from the sunken stern section was "burping" to the surface.

56

The tanker *SE Graham* burns in the water after its collision with the *SS Gulfoil* in the East Passage of Narragansett Bay off Newport, Rhode Island, at 6:45 a.m., August 7, 1958.

Sixteen crew members, including the master of the *Gulfoil*, were burned to death, many trapped below decks in the crew quarters. Several others were missing, while thirty-four were saved from the burning ship and the water by the Coast Guard cutter *Laurel*.

The explosions and fire resulting from the collision caused the worst marine disaster in the northeast since the sinking of the *Andrea Doria*.

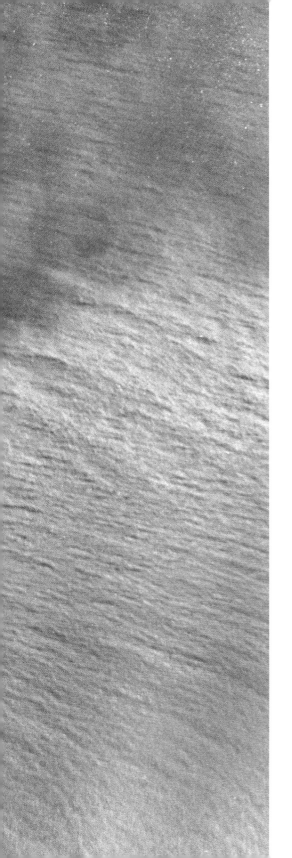

The mid-ship holds of the freighter *Key Largo* (left) are on fire, September 1973. The fire was discovered in holds Three and Four while the ship was en route from New Orleans to Gulfport, Mississippi.

As the fire spread out of control to the engine room and forward to the bridge structure, the freighter was beached and the crew evacuated 50 miles below New Orleans near the town of Myrtle Grove on the Mississippi River. Nearby residents were evacuated from the area.

Coast Guard helicopters and seven other vessels tried to fight the blaze, but neither water nor hundreds of air-dropped 55-lb. chemical bundles could extinguish it.

The heat from the fire melted the superstructure of the *Key Largo* and rendered the ship a total loss.

A Coast Guard crewman watches an HH-3F helicopter drop dry chemicals on the deck of the burning Key Largo.

The fire is not completely out, but the extent of the damage is obvious. Extreme heat has not just blistered the hull, but melted it. The ship was a complete write-off.

March 1964. The Panamanian freighter *M/V Beth* burns ninety miles south/southwest of Santo Domingo after her cargo of lubricating oils and chemicals caught fire on a voyage from Port Arthur, Texas to Martinique.

An HU-16E Albatross flying from the San Juan, Puerto Rico Coast Guard station located the burning ship and its crew, which had taken to the ship's lifeboats. A radio was parachuted to the men in the boats.

A Liberian freighter *World Jonquil* was diverted to the scene and recovered twenty survivors in good condition. Later the Coast Guard cutter *Aurora* removed those survivors and transported them to San Juan.

July 1966. Coast Guard officers aboard the cutter Spencer (above) watch as the British tanker M/V Alva Cape is brought into range of the ship's five-inch guns, which will attempt to sink the tanker before its dangerous naptha cargo can explode. The Alva Cape collided with the American tanker S.S. Texaco Massachusetts while en route to Newark Bay from India. The "killing ground" was an area of the Atlantic 110 miles southeast of New York Harbor.

The spent shell casings on the foredeck of the cutter testify to the number fired at the doomed ship. After some sixty rounds, the Alva Cape was burning fiercely, and in a matter of hours had been consumed to the waterline and sunk.

In addition to the explosions caused by the collision in June, the tanker exploded again during tank cleaning operations two weeks afterward. Thirty-seven men were killed in these two explosions, after which the ship was ordered destroyed. At right, black smoke from burning chemicals arches high into the atmosphere.

February 1942. The ocean liner *Normandie* was at Pier 88 in New York being refitted into a troop transport ship. Welding operations ignited a small fire that went unnoticed. By the time the firewatchers spot the fire it is out of control. In an attempt to extinguish the blaze, firefighters flood the ship with water. The huge volume of water distributes unevenly, and the big ship rolls slowly over on her port side.

December 1968. The *SS Manchester Miller*'s cargo holds astern catch fire while it sits at the East River Pier, New York City.

July 1964. The 304-foot French cargo ship M/V *Marquette* lies burning in the North Atlantic some 800 miles southeast of Cape Race, Newfoundland. A crewman of the Coast Guard's C-130 Hercules aircraft stands in the open doorway observing whether the two 20-man liferafts and portable radio he just dropped to the surviving crew has been reached. Some of the 25-man crew have scrambled into one of the rafts.

The distress call from the *Marquette* had come in at 9:45 a.m. on the 21st. "SOS...fire on board...need assistance." The Eastern Area Rescue Coordination Center in New York received the radio message relayed from the Coast Guard cutter *Duane*. Another cutter, the *Campbell*, was sent for recue. Additionally, Coast Guard aircraft which were on International Ice Patrol duties over the Grand Banks were diverted to assist the rescue operation.

Three hours after the SOS, Coast Guard aircraft located the burning vessel and reported it was burning extensively from the waterline to the superstructure. The French ore carrier *Pentellina*, the closest vessel to the *Marquette*, diverted to the scene and by 2 p.m. had picked up the survivors from liferafts. After the fire had been extinguished and cooled, the *Pentellina* took the *Marquette* in tow for the Azores.

March 1957. The fiercely burning Navy Tanker *Mission of San Francisco* sinks in the Delaware River near New Castle, Delaware after being severed in a collision with the Liberian-registered freighter *Elna II*. Ten men from the Navy ship were killed in the explosion and fires. Fifty-nine others were plucked from the water and from the separated decks of the tanker. Five hours after the incident, the *Mission of San Francisco* sank in the river.

WEATHER

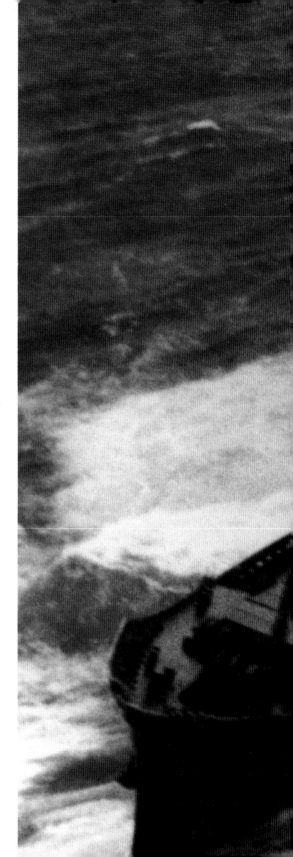

One of the fiercest midwinter storms of the 1950s raged off the Atlantic coast in February of 1952. The Coast Guard was stretched to its maximum rescue capacity even before the full brunt of the storm centered off Cape Cod on February 18. As the barometer fell, near-hurricane winds arose, the seas were wild with 50-foot waves, and a blizzard-level snowfall began. The Coast Guard knew that there was at least one tanker caught in the storm, and by accident discovered a second. Both the 520-foot tanker *Fort Mercer* (pictured above) bound for Portland, Maine, and the 520-foot tanker *Pendleton*, bound for Boston, were pummeled by the storm to such an extent that each broke in two, setting off one of the most remarkable Coast Guard rescues in history.

It was incredible that two ships of this type, which had proven highly durable, would both crack in half within thirty miles of each other at virtually the same time. A single disaster of this magnitude would have taxed the Coast Guard's capabilities; two was a monumental challenge.

A flotilla of rescue ships were immediately dispatched to the area. Despite the

Left: The bow section of the Fort Mercer *begins to sink beneath the waves.*

strong horizontal snowfall, seaplanes were invited to try their luck at aerial reconnaissance. Even small open motor-lifeboats began bouncing over the huge waves to try to reach the stricken ships. A cargo carrier, the *Short Splice*, had been running before the storm, and was nearest to the disaster when her radar operator noticed that the single blip that had been the *Fort Mercer* had become two blips. The *Short Splice* diverted to a position off the severed stern section of the *Fort Mercer*, but was helpless to assist until the storm abated.

Surviving crewmen of both ships were huddled on the bow and stern ends of their ships, and in the howling winds were floating in four separate sections far apart from each other. Their situation looked hopeless.

As ships of all types converged on the disaster zone, they searched through the low visibility for the ship pieces and any sign of life aboard. One by one the sections were located, some very near the beach. The soaked, frightened crewmen could be seen on the decks, hoping for a miracle. In four separate rescue missions, Jacob's ladders were tossed over the sides, and the men started descending to waiting lifeboats. In the pitching seas, with the ladders swinging wildly from four-story-heights, the rescue was extremely hazardous. Some men fell into the sea and were hauled into the boats; others jumped from great heights and crashed onto the decks. Others were lost to the wind and waves.

When it was all over, more than 1,000 men had participated in the rescue. Of the 84 victims, fourteen were dead, 57 were rescued, and thirteen remained on the stern section of the *Fort Mercer* as it was towed into New York for rebuilding.

The tanker Pendleton *aground off Chatham, Massachusetts.*

Coast Guard crewmen frantically pull a rubber liferaft toward them, hoping to send it back for more survivors before the Fort Mercer *sinks.*

Right: The stern section of the Pendleton *the morning after the storm. Thirty-two men escaped down the Jacob's ladder seen hanging over the side of the ship.*

The Finnish tanker *Ragny*, fully loaded with heating oil and en route to Finland from the Bahamas, ran into a severe storm 450 miles north of Bermuda. While the crew was assembled for their evening meal in the stern section, the ship split in two without warning. The lights went out as the men scrambled for evacuation points. In the pitching seas it was impossible to launch the lifeboats. The Coast Guard cutter *Escanaba* arrived to rescue the survivors, but not before the *Ragny*'s crew had spent nearly twenty-four hours drifting in the stern section, wondering whether their half-boat would stay afloat long enough for help to arrive.

Above: The rescue was accomplished in darkness after the seas had abated somewhat.

The Coast Guard cutter Coos Bay, *arriving to rescue the crew of the sinking British motorship* Ambassador, *fires a lifeline to the* Ambassador *crew huddled along the bow rail. The* Coos Bay *joined the Norwegian ship* Fruen, *which had already begun rescue operations the previous day 370 miles south of the outer tip of the Grand Banks in the North Atlantic. Constant rolling from 20 to 30 degrees in 25-foot seas and 40-knot winds made the rescue hazardous. Of the* Ambassador's *crew of 35, fourteen were lost during the* Fruen *rescue; one was lost during the* Coos Bay *rescue; twenty survived.*

Waves driven by 40-knot winds crash against the already-listing Ambassador. *Lifeboats can be seen still in their davits, unable to be launched in the rolling sea. Liferafts were passed by line to the sinking ship; they capsized as waves rolled over the top. Coast Guard crewmen in wetsuits dove over the side to rescue them. All but one was recovered.*

December 1960. Mountainous seas 125 miles due east of Cape Hatteras, North Carolina have broken the American tanker Pine Ridge *in two (left). The bow portion, almost three hundred feet in length but hidden underwater, sinks with a flourish. (Above) A helicopter from the U.S. Navy aircraft carrier* Valley Forge *hovers over the still-floating stern section, onto which all the surviving crew are clinging. Of the 36 crewmen, 28 are rescued. Eight men, including the master and first mate, met their death when the vessel broke in half.*

The fishing trawler Pacific Star *(left and above), on fire and taking on water, is attended by the cutter* Citrus. *The crew is rescued but the salvage effort is frustrated by the fast-building fire. In a very short time the* Pacific Star *rolls over on her port side and sinks.*

The Coast Guard Cutter Point Judith *has rescued the crew and now stands by as the tanker M/V Pacbaronness sinks in the Atlantic.*

COLLISIONS

July 1956. The Swedish ocean liner *Stockholm*, steaming eastward from New York in the dark of night at 11 p.m., in a thick fog off the coast of Nantucket, strikes the Italian ocean liner *Andrea Doria* broadside.

The collision slices a mortal hole in the *Andrea Doria* below the waterline. She begins to list quickly, preventing the lifeboats from being lowered. An urgent SOS goes out, and is responded to by many ships in the area. Over the next ten hours most of the 1500 passengers and crew of the *Andrea Doria* are rescued; maritime historians have called it one of the greatest rescue operations ever mounted.

Ten hours after the collision, the *Andrea Doria* foundered and sank.

The *Stockholm* survived the collision, but with her bow crumpled, and limped back to New York with a Coast Guard escort.

Forty-seven people died on the *Andrea Doria*; five crewmen died on the *Stockholm*.

The Andrea Doria *rolls on her side, just minutes away from sinking after a half day of dramatic rescues.*

Coast Guard airplanes could only fly helplessly over the stricken Italian liner. The Andrea Doria *sank moments after this photograph was taken.*

What do you do in the open Pacific after a severe bow collision? If the seas are calm, and you're not sinking, you do what the Star K is doing— steam in reverse to the nearest repair facility.

September 1972. The Colombia-registered freighter *Republica de Colombia* lists to starboard with the bow of the 520-foot U.S. containership *Transhawaii* pierced through the portside engine room. The two vessels collided twelve miles east of Cape Hatteras, North Carolina.

One man was killed in the accident and four others were injured. An estimated 24,000 gallons of diesel oil spilled from the Colombian freighter, but due to dissipation and sinking did not reach the shore.

The two vessels remained locked together for over 24 hours, drifting first to the northeast, then to the southwest, until they were separated by commercial tug.

Left: This aerial view from a Coast Guard airplane shows the oil slick coming from the holds of the Republica de Colombia.

This photo from a Coast Guard cutter shows the bow of the Fernview *locked into the afterdeck of the tanker* Dynafuel.

This airview shows the full force of the impact. Fire-fighting and rescue ships crowd the bow of the Fernview.

November 1963. In hazy weather, the Norwegian freighter *Fernview* has collided with the tanker *Dynafuel* near the canal entrance to Buzzard's Bay, South Dartmouth, Massachusetts. The freighter's bow has rammed twenty feet into the tanker's afterdeck, through the crew's quarters and almost into the engine room.

Fire erupted in both ships on impact. The major fire was in the *Dynafuel*'s engine room. Foam was flown by helicopter from shore stations to extinguish the blaze.

After considerable effort, the ships were pryed apart. The *Dynafuel* had no chance to remain afloat, and sank stern-first. The *Fernview* was able to limp to port.

No deaths resulted from this mishap, but five men from the *Dynafuel* were injured. Environmental damage was negligible; the *Dynafuel* had been unloaded the previous day.

Right: Coast Guard vessels and an HH-52A helicopter fight a raging fire mainly in the engine room of the American Coastal Tanker Dynafuel.

The 609-foot bulk carrier *Summit Venture* collided in the early morning hours with the bridge supports of the Sunshine Skyway Bridge over Tampa Bay. Some 1200 feet of the bridge collapsed into the Bay below, with morning commuter traffic unaware of the missing span. A Greyhound bus, a truck, and several cars plummeted 140 feet, killing 35 people.

The Norwegian tanker Jalanta *shows the damage that resulted from her collision with the American luxury liner* Constitution *near the New York Harbor entrance in March 1959. A 135-foot bow section was severed from the ship, but managed to stay afloat.*

The Jalanta's bow lies on its starboard side at a shipyard in Hoboken, New Jersey. There were no injuries in this collision.

With the Brooklyn Bridge rising in the background, the sheared bow of the tanker *Empress Bay* slips beneath the waters of New York's East River. The ill-fated tanker collided with the freighter *Nebraska* on the morning of June 25, 1958. *The Empress Bay*'s 280,000 gallons of gasoline erupted on impact, engulfing both ships in a ball of fire. The ships locked together and drifted, still burning, under the Manhattan Bridge, where the flames caused damage to high-tension wires. Several hours later the ships sank in 55 feet of water, and remained there until commercial salvage operations were completed three months later.

Two men from the 55-man complement of both ships lost their lives in this accident.

(Left and above) Navigating bridge spans have always been the trickiest part of commercial barge traffic, especially on rivers. Here a towboat with two shell barges has collided with the Pass Manchac Bridge, knocking out two spans. One person was killed in this incident.

The aftermath of the collision between the M/V *Hong Kong Truth* and the global tanker *Pioneer Valley* on May 26, 1969. As can be seen, damage on the *Hong Kong Truth* extended from the 20-foot draught mark ten frames to the starboard side and six frames on the port side. The vessel was moored at San Francisco awaiting repairs.

The *Hong Kong Truth* was bound from Melbourne, Australia to Vancouver, B.C. when, in a dense fog, she rammed the *Pioneer Valley* bow-first approximately five miles off the California coast south of San Francisco.

The *Pioneer Valley* was ripped on her port side at an empty compartment. There were no casualties, no injuries, and no oil leakage. Both ships proceeded under their own power to San Francisco escorted by the Coast Guard cutter *Point Barrow*.

After the fire is extinguished, investigators observe the twenty-foot hole in the side of the Esso Brussels.

The cargo on the Sea Witch *is incinerated.*

Coast Guard personnel oversee the fire-fighting operations directed on the Sea Witch *(in background).*

June 1973. In New York Harbor an oil tanker, the *Esso Brussels*, is rammed by a containership, the *Sea Witch*, while it is at anchor off Stapleton, Staten Island, just north of the Verrazano-Narrows Bridge. The collision leaves a 20-foot-wide gash in the tanker's port side. The resulting fire and explosion send fireballs up to the bridge's road surface, and ignite the general cargo on the deck of the *Sea Witch*. Afire and locked together from the impact, the two ships float two miles south into Gravesend Bay near Brooklyn.

Eight men are killed instantly in the explosion, and eight more are missing and presumed dead. Failure of the steering mechanism of the *Sea Witch* is blamed for the ship's veering off course.

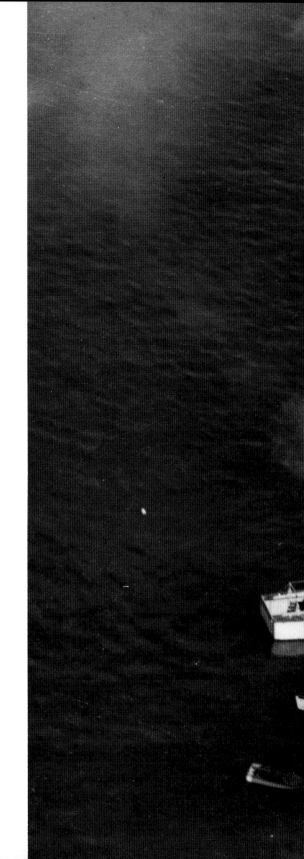

RESCUES

The Soviet Factory vessel, **Grigory Lysenko**, *radioed for medical assistance when a crewman was seriously injured on April 2, 1967. A Coast Guard helicopter is just arriving to transport the man to a hospital.*

April 1967. The Soviet ship *Grigory Lysenko*, mother ship to a small fleet of Russian fishing vessels, is under way 70 miles south of Montauk Point, New York when an on-board injury provokes a call to the U.S. Coast Guard for emergency medical assistance.

A helo is dispatched, along with an observation airplane which circles the 20,000-ton vessel throughout the rescue operation.

After a touch-down in a very confined space, the helo successfully completes its mission.

The helo is now secured to the deck.

Soviet fishing trawlers moor alongside the mother ship.

Crewman Fernando Mena clings to a life ring, as seen from a Coast Guard spotter plane.

September 1965. A crewman has fallen overboard from the Panamanian freighter *Humboldt* while 230 miles south of Bermuda in the open sea. An emergency call to the Coast Guard brings an Albatross aircraft to the area to search for the fallen man. For four hours the crewman swims without the aid of a life jacket. The Albatross then spots him from the air, drops two smoke floats to mark his position, and directs the *Humboldt*'s rescue operation. A lifeboat is lowered and the crewman is soon recovered, still swimming strongly despite his length of time in the water. The *Humboldt* then continued on its voyage to Tampa, Florida.

September 1958. A flotilla of Coast Guard vessels (above left) takes on the double duty of keeping curious boatmen away, and searching for survivors from a New Jersey Central Railroad passenger train which has gone through an open bridge and fallen into Newark Bay.

Completely submerged are two locomotives and two passenger cars, one empty and one filled with about 50 people. A third car which carried 30 persons is partially in the water, leaning against a concrete bridge pillar. The last two cars remained on the tracks (above). The train was en route from Bay Head to Jersey City, New Jersey.

Helicopters, airplanes, and rescue boats were immediately sent to the area. The channel was closed to navigation, and divers began their grim search for the dead and injured.

119

At first sign of daylight, the crippled airplane swooped low over the Coast Guard boat to signal the beginning of the landing.

Commander William Earle talked the pilot down to the surface.

The pilot lands perfectly on a calm sea.

October 1956. The Pan Am Stratocruiser "Sovereign of the Skies" was flying its normal route from Honolulu to San Francisco with 24 passengers and seven crew members aboard. At 3:20 a.m., halfway across the Pacific Ocean, just past the point of no return and still over 1,000 miles from her destination, the plane's number one engine and number four engine failed almost simultaneously. There was nothing to do but ditch the airplane.

On the ocean below, performing weather patrol duty, was the Coast Guard cutter *Pontchartrain*. A communications link was established with the crippled airplane. The pilot, Richard Ogg, decided to try to hold his airplane in the air until daylight in order to give the passengers a better chance to escape the ship. The *Pontchartrain* prepared for the emergency by illuminating a landing path on the ocean with water flares, laid a two-mile path of fire-retardant foam on the water, readied fire hoses, and lowered all available lifeboats. On the plane, the passengers drilled in lifesaving techniques.

By 8:13 a.m. the ocean was calm and 74 degrees. Commander William Earle talked the pilot down, and Captain Ogg executed a perfect belly landing. Within twenty minutes of hitting the water all passengers and crew were out of the plane and safely aboard the *Pontchartrain*. A minute later the plane sank.

The battered lifeboat (above) from which five of the only six survivors of the sinking of the German training barque Pamir *is taken in tow by the Coast Guard cutter* Absecon. *The* Pamir, *with a crew of 87, including 52 Merchant Marine cadets, was caught in Hurricane Carrie 550 miles southwest of the Azores in September of 1957.*

Right: The lifeboat crew of the Coast Guard cutter Absecon *finds and rescues the sixth and last survivor of the* Pamir *sinking. The* Absecon *was responding to the distress call of the* Pamir, *which had said it had lost its sails and was listing 45 degrees.*

The charter fishing vessel *NORA V* took on water from a hole below her water line on the port bow while on a fishing excursion off Murderkill Neck, Delaware. The boat capsized, spilling all nine passengers and crew into the water. Responding to the *NORA V* distress call, the Coast Guard sent a helicopter and numerous boats to the rescue. Three passengers drowned in this mishap.

Right: The Coast Guard ship Gentian *prepares to haul aboard the capsized* NORA V.

A Coast Guard patrol boat approaches the capsized NORA V.

One of the NORA V *survivors is rescued.*

When onboard medical emergencies call for quick evacuation and a helicopter is not available, there are other ways to get people off a ship. Here, a crewman with a ruptured appendix is lowered in a sling called a "stokes litter" over the side of the Norwegian cargo ship *Gausdal* to the Coast Guard cutter *Point Barrow*. This medical evacuation took place off San Francisco Lightship.

Dedicated to the men and women of the United States Coast Guard, whose heroic deeds and daring rescues set the standard throughout the world for maritime service excellence.